CAN YOU SURVIVE

DEATH-DEFYING

OCEAN

ENCOUNTERS?

An Interactive
Wilderness Adventure

by Allison Lassieur

CAPSTONE PRESS
a capstone imprint

Published by Capstone Press, an imprint of Capstone
1710 Roe Crest Drive, North Mankato, Minnesota 56003
capstonepub.com

Library of Congress Cataloging-in-Publication Data
Names: Lassieur, Allison, author.
Title: Can you survive death-defying ocean encounters? : an interactive wilderness adventure
/ by Allison Lassieur.
Description: North Mankato, Minnesota : Capstone Press, 2023. | Series: You choose. Wild
encounters | Includes bibliographical references. | Audience: Ages 8-12 | Audience: Grades
4-6 | Summary: "Could you survive being stranded at sea? Imagine encountering a barracuda
in the Caribbean Sea, a jellyfish in Australia's Great Barrier Reef, or a humpback whale in the
Arctic Ocean. How far would you be willing to go to save your own life? Would it work? Flip
through these pages to find out!"— Provided by publisher.
Identifiers: LCCN 2022009483 (print) | LCCN 2022009484 (ebook) | ISBN
9781666338003 (hardcover) | ISBN 9781666338010 (paperback) | ISBN 9781666338027
(pdf) Subjects: LCSH: Wilderness survival—Juvenile literature. | Survival at sea—Juvenile
literature. | Marine animals—Juvenile literature.
Classification: LCC GV200.5 .L273 2023 (print) | LCC GV200.5 (ebook) | DDC
613.6/9—dc23/eng/20220225
LC record available at https://lccn.loc.gov/2022009483
LC ebook record available at https://lccn.loc.gov/2022009484

Editor: Mandy Robbins; Designer: Heidi Thompson; Media Researchers: Jo Miller and
Pam Mitsakos; Production Specialist: Tori Abraham

Image Credits
Alamy: Anthony Pierce, 98; Getty Images: Cavan Images, 19, dottedhippo, 80,
imageBROKER/Norbert Probst, 39; Shutterstock: bearacreative, 46, Chainarong
Phrammanee, 50, Chase Dekker, 93, Christian Musat, 85, Connie Kouwenhoven, 63, Digital
Storm, Cover, Dotted Yeti, 91, Ethan Daniels, 25, 88, Fiona Ayerst, 30, frantisekhojdysz,
112, Henry and Laura Whittaker, 35, Islandjems - Jemma Craig, 65, John A. Anderson, 26,
korkeng, design element, throughout, Michael Bogner, 105, Miles Away Photography, 96,
mishelo0, 55, Ocean Image Photography, 22, Tory Kallman, 76, wildestanimal, 48

TABLE OF CONTENTS

ENCOUNTERS AT SEA!

YOU find yourself exploring the ocean. Threats lie hidden everywhere. Water stretches out past you. And dangerous sea creatures lurk at every turn. You could face stingrays, jellyfish, and even sharks. You never know what you might find—or what might find you.

What will you do when you come face-to-face with a deadly ocean creature? Will you flee? Will you hide? Do you have what it takes to survive? YOU CHOOSE which paths to take. Your choices will guide the story and decide—will you live or die?

• Turn the page to begin your adventure.

CHAPTER 1

AN OCEAN ADVENTURE

The world's oceans have always interested you. They are filled with beautiful creatures, dangerous predators, and sunken treasure. You've read everything you could find about sea life and watched every documentary on ocean animals, famous sailors, and sunken ships. You've imagined watching a whale glide past or swimming with dolphins. You know you would remember it as long as you live.

• Turn the page.

Finally, after years of learning and dreaming, it's your turn for an ocean adventure! Your biggest concern is running into a deadly ocean animal. You know most sea creatures aren't dangerous to humans. Often, ocean animal encounters are safe. But sometimes things don't go as planned.

You also know the basic rule for safely encountering wild ocean creatures. Don't do anything to cause the animal's behavior to change. If an animal suddenly swims faster, or darts in a different direction, that could be a sign that it is stressed or afraid. A good rule of thumb is to keep your distance.

You've learned all you can to prepare yourself for your adventure on the high seas. Where will you choose to go?

- To explore shipwrecks in the Caribbean, turn to page 11.
- To travel to the Great Barrier Reef, turn to page 41.
- To study Arctic marine ecosystems, turn to page 67.

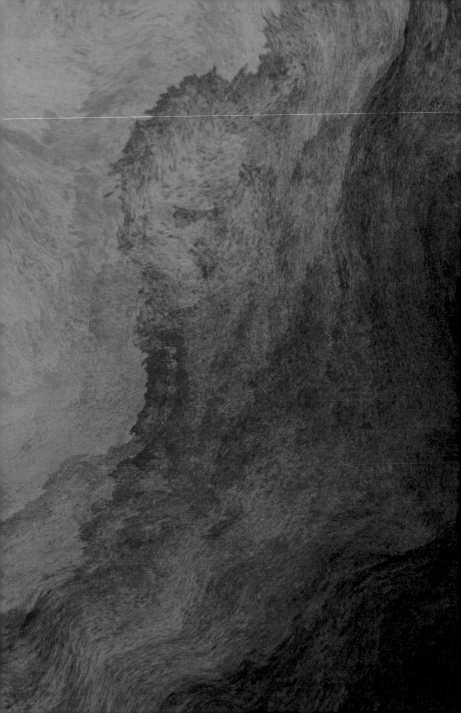

CHAPTER 2

EXPLORING THE CARIBBEAN

From the time you learned how to dive, you've dreamed of exploring shipwrecks. There's nothing more thrilling than pulling on scuba gear and diving through the remains of ships that have been swallowed by the sea. Shipwrecks are also home to some stunning undersea life. It's almost as much fun to encounter wild sea animals as it is to dive.

• Turn the page.

You do months of research to decide where you're going for your next diving adventure. You settle on two locations. One is in the waters around Cuba. Hundreds of ships have wrecked there, so it's a good place to explore. The other is Amelia Island, off the coast of Florida. A treasure ship called the *San Miguel* is reported to have wrecked there in 1715. Maybe you'll find real treasure!

These areas are filled with beautiful coral reefs and wildlife too. Which will you choose?

• To explore the Cuban coast, go to page 13.
• To dive around Amelia Island, turn to page 29.

Traveling to Cuba isn't easy. For many years, Americans were not allowed to visit Cuba. Today, the rules have changed. Americans can visit, but getting permission from the United States government to go there is difficult. After many weeks, you finally have all the paperwork you need. You're ready to go!

You choose the island nation of Saint Lucia as your home base. The area has a beautiful coral reef.

A coral reef is a huge underwater structure filled with living animals called corals. Corals often look like plants, swaying gently in the water. They come in many bright, beautiful colors. Diving in a coral reef can be an amazing experience.

The waters around Saint Lucia also have many shipwrecks. All kinds of marine animals live in these old wrecks.

• Turn the page.

Early one morning, a boat takes you several miles offshore. You dive into the water with your metal detector. Soon, one of Cuba's famous coral reefs appears. It's even more beautiful than you imagined! Colorful fish dart through the coral. Their feathery fins sway in the current.

You don't notice the large fish that glides toward you. It's as long as you are tall. Its narrow, silvery body makes it almost invisible in the water. Several rows of sharp teeth stick out of its needle-like mouth. It swims past you and then turns around. It seems to be staring you down.

- To stay and watch the fish, go to page 15.
- To move to a different part of the coral reef, turn to page 21.

This fish is easily over 5 feet long and at least 100 pounds. It disappears into the reef. Before you have a chance to relax, it appears again. But this time, it has brought along some friends. They all have the same sleek, tube-like body and sharp teeth, but they're smaller.

That's when you realize what kind of fish they are. They are barracudas, one of the most dangerous predators in the Caribbean. If you dive down farther, they might leave you alone. Or you could stay still and hope they ignore you.

• To dive deeper, turn to page 16.
• To stay put, turn to page 19.

You don't remember much about barracudas. You know they're fast. Right now, they're circling slowly, checking you out. You don't *think* they attack humans, but you don't want to find out. Slowly, you dive farther down, hoping they'll leave you alone. As you drop lower in the water, your underwater watch glints in the sunlight. Suddenly, the large fish dashes toward you in a stunning burst of speed.

• To attempt to swim away, go to page 17.
• To defend yourself, turn to page 18.

Too late, you remember that barracudas are drawn to shiny objects. It quickly attacks your arm. Its teeth pierce your skin. A burst of pain rips through you. You swing at the fish as hard as you can. It lets go, and you kick to the surface. Thankfully, it doesn't follow you.

Once you're back on the boat, you look at your injury. There's a long, deep gash across your forearm. You definitely need stitches. But it could have been so much worse. Your team brings you to the closest hospital for medical attention.

Back in town, a doctor stitches up the wound. She says it's not a good idea to dive again any time soon. Your wound could get infected from the germs in the ocean water. For now, your underwater adventure is over.

THE END

To follow another path, turn to page 8.
To learn more about sharing the ocean, turn to page 101.

Before it can attack, you swing at the fish and knock it away. Your heart pounds as the fish darts back. Then it returns and watches you cautiously. You swim backward, keeping an eye on the big barracuda. Finally, the fish disappears from view.

You make your way to the dive boat and tell the captain your story. He laughs.

"Barracudas aren't dangerous to humans unless they see shiny objects—like your watch. They might mistake it for a smaller fish and try to take a bite." You're lucky you got away unscathed.

Your encounter has made your heart pound. You've had enough diving for the day. Maybe tomorrow you'll continue your treasure hunt—in a different part of the coral reef.

THE END

To follow another path, turn to page 8.
To learn more about sharing the ocean, turn to page 101.

You stay motionless in the water as the fish swim slowly around you. You don't think barracudas are usually dangerous. But you have heard of a few times they've attacked humans. Maybe if you stay still, they'll just ignore you.

• Turn the page.

You hold your breath. Then the big one swims toward you. You brace for an attack. Your mind races, wondering what you'll do if it attacks.

Instead, the huge fish gently nudges your shoulder. You hold your position. Then it swims away. The smaller fish follow.

Once you've calmed down, you continue exploring. You swim through schools of fish. You see colorful starfish and sea sponges. Huge elkhorn coral rise from the reef. They get their name because they look like enormous horns.

After a couple of hours exploring, you're ready to quit for the day. You head back to the dive boat, excited about all you've encountered and looking forward to what the rest of your trip will bring.

THE END

To follow another path, turn to page 8.
To learn more about sharing the ocean, turn to page 101.

You're not sure, but this might be a barracuda, with its long tube-like body and razor-sharp teeth. Even though you can't identify the fish, it doesn't look like something to take a chance with. Quickly, you swim away.

In the distance, you see the outline of a huge shadow on the ocean floor. Your heart skips a beat. It's definitely an old shipwreck! You've got to explore it!

Then you check the gauge on the scuba tanks. You're getting low on air. If you're not careful, you could run out of air if you get trapped or lost inside the shipwreck. Should you just explore the exterior or risk going inside?

• To explore the exterior of the shipwreck, turn to page 22.
• To check out the inside, turn to page 24.

You don't want to run out of air, so you explore the top, or deck, of the ship. This must be the *Nuevo Mortera*. Your dive boat captain told you about it. You can make out the old cannons on the deck. They're covered with coral. A school of parrotfish darts past you. Their colors flash in the light.

Right behind them, several large fish appear. They're bull sharks! They're are among the deadliest sharks in the world, though they rarely attack humans.

As you consider your next move, another diver splashes into the water. It's the dive boat captain. To your surprise, he starts feeding the sharks! One by one, they swim past and grab a fish from his hand. He offers a fish to you. You're too nervous to take it. You motion to the boat, and he follows.

Back on the boat, he tells you that he's an experienced shark feeder. He does a shark feeding show for tourists. He has never been injured. Watching him feed the sharks was incredible, but you don't ever want to do it.

THE END

To follow another path, turn to page 8.
To learn more about sharing the ocean, turn to page 101.

You've always wanted to see the inside of a shipwreck! You duck under fallen beams and gaze around in wonder. You spot a tiny red seahorse. It's the size of your pinky finger. It grips a coral with its tail. Fish pop out of the dim shadows and speed away. A huge spiny lobster makes its way along the bottom. Then it disappears into a hole in the wreck.

Watching the lobster makes you hungry. The dive captain says it's legal to catch lobster for eating, and it will be dinnertime by the time you get back to land. If you caught it, what a feast you'd have! But catching that lobster means swimming into that dark hole. You check the air gauge. You'll be out of oxygen soon.

• To grab the lobster, go to page 25.
• To return to the boat, turn to page 28.

You can almost taste your lobster dinner as you swim into the hole. It's not completely dark in here, but it is hard to see. You spot the movement of the lobster. You reach out, making sure to stay clear of its huge claws.

• Turn the page.

A sudden searing pain rips through your hand! Frantically, you swim out of the hole and see a 2-foot-long green moray eel clamped to your thumb. The pain is almost unbearable. Not only are a moray's teeth super sharp, but they point backward to better hold their prey. Moray eels also have a second set of jaws that helps them grip prey even harder.

It was a terrible idea to go swimming into that hole. Moray eels lurk in dark spaces, waiting for prey to swim by. Panicked and in pain, you kick toward the surface.

Just before you get there, the eel lets go. Your thumb is gushing blood. You climb up the ladder, yelling for help. The dive boat captain stops the bleeding and races to shore.

The emergency room doctor who stitches you up says you're lucky that you still have your thumb. It will be a long time before you can dive again. Even then, you're not sure you'll want to.

THE END

To follow another path, turn to page 8.
To learn more about sharing the ocean, turn to page 101.

As tempting as a lobster dinner sounds, you're not about to swim into a dark hole. Anything could be in there, maybe even a moray eel. They hide inside dark crevices and holes in coral reefs, waiting for prey. This nasty-looking fish has a mouthful of sharp teeth and causes painful bites. One might mistake you for prey if you come too close.

The alarm on your scuba tank goes off, warning you that your air supply is almost gone. As you swim back over the wreck, you spot another spiny lobster among the coral. You'd love a lobster dinner, but you head to the surface empty-handed. You would rather leave it alone in its beautiful ocean home.

THE END

To follow another path, turn to page 8.
To learn more about sharing the ocean, turn to page 101.

During the 1700s, Spanish treasure ships sailed from the New World to Europe. They were loaded with gold and gems.

In the summer of 1715, a fleet of 11 treasure ships left Havana, Cuba. As the ships neared the Florida coast, a hurricane struck. The wooden vessels broke apart in the storm.

These sunken ships took tons of treasure to the bottom of the ocean. One of the ships was the *San Miguel*. Modern-day treasure hunters think it was the most valuable ship in the fleet. No one is sure where the *San Miguel* sank. One possible location is near Amelia Island. That's where you're going to start your search.

You flick on the metal detector and begin the treasure search. After an hour, you've found a rusty screwdriver and a broken watch, but no Spanish treasure.

• Turn the page.

You're about to give up. Then a sleek grey form swims slowly through the dim water toward you. It has to be a shark! If it is, you should get out of here fast.

On the other hand, you've never seen a shark on a dive before. And many sharks aren't dangerous to humans anyway. If you keep still, it likely won't bother you.

• To stay where you are, go to page 31.
• To swim away, turn to page 36.

You freeze, in the hopes of seeing a marine animal you've never seen before. Your heart thumps in your chest as it comes closer. This is no harmless shark. It's a tiger shark!

Tiger sharks are one of the "big three" predator shark species. This group also includes great white sharks and bull sharks.

The tiger shark starts to circle. You freeze, terrified. The shark swims toward you!

Just as you accept that you are facing certain death, an enormous fish appears. It's a goliath grouper. Wow, this fish is huge! It's easily over 300 pounds, with rough skin and huge spiky fins sticking out of its back.

Before the shark can attack you, the grouper swallows it in one giant gulp! Only the shark's tail sticks out of the grouper's mouth. It's flapping like crazy.

• Turn the page.

Unless they see you as a meal, goliath groupers are gentle, calm fish. They aren't a threat to humans. Seeing one on a dive is a rare treat. Watching one eat a shark is almost unheard of. It saved your life. As scary as this was, you are glad you stayed still. If you had swam away, you would never have seen it. The huge fish slowly disappears.

• To go back to treasure hunting, go to page 33.
• To follow the goliath grouper, turn to page 34.

Once your heartbeat slows down, you return to the treasure hunt. After a while, you spot something interesting on the ocean floor. The metal detector's alarm goes off. You carefully wave the sand away. You uncover a long, thin object covered with a hard crust. What could it be? It's some old object that sank with a ship.

Back in town you take the object to a local museum. It turns out to be a silver spoon. It's more than 200 years old. It's not the golden treasure you hoped for. But it is a cool find, nonetheless. You offer the spoon to the museum. The museum director is happy to add it to their collection. You start planning your next dive. Hopefully, there will be fewer sharks and more treasure.

THE END

To follow another path, turn to page 8.
To learn more about sharing the ocean, turn to page 101.

You're amazed by this gentle giant, so you follow it. It leads you to a large school of giant groupers that have gathered around a shipwreck. They swim calmly through the ruins. Suddenly, booming sounds ring through the water. You're shocked when you realize the groupers are making these noises.

You've heard of this! The fish are here to mate. Goliath groupers are very endangered. You don't want to disturb them by investigating the ship nearby.

Carefully, you swim away. They watch you but leave you alone. After a few minutes, you head for the surface. You'll never forget this experience. It was even better than a treasure hunt.

THE END

To follow another path, turn to page 8.
To learn more about sharing the ocean, turn to page 101.

You don't want to find out if that fish is a shark or not. You swim away as fast as you can!

You spend the next hour searching the sandy ocean bottom for treasure but come up empty.

On your way back to the ship, you notice a large shadow moving above you. It's a school of spotted eagle rays! Their beautiful fins flap gracefully in the water. Most are very large. Some can grow up to 16 feet long, including their tails.

Despite the venomous barbs on their tails, you doubt eagle rays are dangerous to people. They're very shy and hard to get close to. One seems friendly, though. It swims toward you.

• To reach out to the ray, go to page 37.
• To cross your arms and let it go by, turn to page 38.

You had pet one of these at an aquarium once. This ray seems friendly. You reach out to touch it as it passes. But this is no captive ray. It's wild. Instantly, it whips its tail around and stings you in the arm.

You rush back to the dive boat. Your arm is throbbing in pain. The captain removes the stingers and cleans the cut with soap and water. By the time you reach the shore, your arm is red and swollen. You feel sick, but you're not going to die. After a few days, the swelling goes down.

You're ready to go out on one more treasure hunt before your trip ends. This time, you're going to keep your hands to yourself.

THE END

To follow another path, turn to page 8.
To learn more about sharing the ocean, turn to page 101.

Being so close to such a beautiful creature is exciting. You don't want to scare it away. You cross your arms and stay still. Slowly, it swims past and rejoins the school. You watch them fade into the blue water.

Another hour goes by, and you don't find any treasure. You thought you'd be disappointed at not finding gold or jewels. But the wonderful ocean creatures you've seen today make up for it. You happily return to the boat. You're ready to try again tomorrow.

THE END

To follow another path, turn to page 8.
To learn more about sharing the ocean, turn to page 101.

CHAPTER 3

GREAT BARRIER REEF ENCOUNTERS

The Great Barrier Reef is one of the seven natural wonders of the world. It is the largest coral reef on Earth. It can even be seen from space!

The reef is home to some of the most interesting and unusual ocean creatures on Earth. It's also in danger due to climate change and pollution. You want to see the reef while it's still healthy.

• Turn the page.

After years of planning and saving, your dream has come true! You'll spend a week living on board a boat and exploring the Great Barrier Reef.

The first day on the boat is clear and beautiful. Much of the coral reef is in shallow water. These areas of the reef are closer to sunlight. It's easy to see their vibrant colors and ocean life. Other parts of the reef are in deeper water. The best way to see those areas is to scuba dive.

Today, one group wants to scuba dive in deep water. Another group decides to go snorkeling in shallower water. Which will you do?

• To join the scuba diving group, go to page 43.
• To go snorkeling, turn to page 54.

You want to see more than what's just below the surface of the water. The reef is home to thousands of species of animals. Who knows what kinds of sea creatures you'll encounter?

After a few minutes, your group reaches the ocean floor. You carefully swim through rocks and corals.

You're amazed at the beauty. A school of black and white zebra fish shoot past. A leatherjacket fish, with its bright yellow and blue scales, calmly swims by.

A bit farther ahead, the group has gathered around something. You're a little curious as to what they've found. But it could also be fun to explore another area of the reef.

• To see what they're looking at, turn to page 44.
• To swim off on your own, turn to page 50.

You come closer to see what they're all looking at. It's a giant clam! They can live 100 years and grow to more than 400 pounds. This one is so big, it could probably swallow you whole. But giant clams are no danger to humans. The only thing they eat is plankton. They are tiny creatures that float in the water. You're thrilled to see a giant clam up close.

Everyone takes photos and videos. Then it's time to keep exploring.

You move off on your own. Soon, a large fish comes into view. It has enormous, delicate fins and spines that float as it moves. Its body is covered with brown stripes. It looks familiar, but you can't quite remember what kind of fish this is.

• To get closer, go to page 45.
• To watch from a distance, turn to page 47.

The fish moves gently through the corals. It ignores you. It might be a lionfish. They are an invasive species in the Gulf of Mexico and the Caribbean. That means they live in areas they aren't supposed to be in. But lionfish are native to this area. It's okay for them to be here.

As it swims by, it brushes your hand with its spines. Suddenly, blinding pain shoots up your arm. You forgot that lionfish were venomous!

You can barely stand the pain as you struggle to get back to the boat. By now, your hand is red and swollen. You're sweaty, and your arm is tingling.

The captain uses tweezers to remove the lionfish spine from your skin. Then he washes the wound with hot water. He gives you medicine for the pain.

• Turn the page.

A few hours later, you're feeling better. A lionfish sting isn't deadly. But your arm is going to hurt for a few days. You're also going to miss out on the rest of the dive. You'll think twice about touching wildlife in the future.

THE END

To follow another path, turn to page 8.
To learn more about sharing the ocean, turn to page 101.

This might be a lionfish. You've seen pictures of them. You definitely don't want to get close to it. It's one of the most venomous fish on the Great Barrier Reef. A sting from it probably won't kill you, but it will really hurt. You watch it swim away. Then you head to another part of the reef.

For the next hour, you swim through the coral reef. You take photos and videos of all the wonders. The beautiful colors take your breath away.

After a while, the other divers begin swimming back to the boat. But you're not quite ready to leave. Soon, you're the only person left in the water. A large shape swims toward you. You instantly know it's some kind of shark. Your heart skips a beat. Time to get out and go back to the boat! But wait. Not all sharks are deadly to humans. What kind of shark is this?

• To go back to the boat, turn to page 48.
• To stay and try to identify the shark, turn to page 49.

Some divers love to swim with sharks. You're not one of them. Quickly, you swim up to the surface and climb aboard the boat. The other passengers are jealous that you saw a shark. You describe it to them. They agree that it was probably a harmless lemon shark. Part of you wishes you had watched it longer. The other part is glad you left when you did.

THE END

To follow another path, turn to page 8.
To learn more about sharing the ocean, turn to page 101.

This shark isn't very big. Its skin has a yellow color to it. That means it's probably a lemon shark. Lemon sharks are not dangerous to humans. Relieved, you carefully swim alongside the shark. You get a few great selfies to post online later. Everyone will be so jealous that you swam with a shark!

The lemon shark disappears, and you head for the surface. Suddenly, another shark appears. With a sickening feeling, you realize this isn't the calm lemon shark. It's a great white shark! Great white sharks are at the top of the deadliest shark list. It's rare to see a great white shark here. As you frantically swim away, the shark takes a bite out of one of your swim fins. You race to the surface and collapse on the deck. You tell everyone what happened. No one is jealous of this ocean encounter.

THE END

To follow another path, turn to page 8.
To learn more about sharing the ocean, turn to page 101.

You want to find your own adventure, so you swim away. Soon, you see neon-yellow butterfly fish. Graceful angelfish glide past. Orange clownfish wander through the white tentacles of sea anemones.

Something huge slowly appears in the hazy water. It's the biggest fish you've ever seen! It's a whale shark.

Whale sharks are a species of shark, but they aren't predators. They get their name from their huge size. Most whale sharks are the size of a school bus. They can grow to be about 18 to 32 feet long. They can weigh up to 20 tons.

Whale sharks look different from other sharks, too. Not only are they bigger, but they have flat heads and broad mouths.

You pause, wondering what to do. You're not sure you want to get too close to any kind of wildlife, much less an animal this big.

- To stay a safe distance away, turn to page 52.
- To approach the whale shark, turn to page 53.

By now, the other divers have come to see the whale shark. Everyone keeps a safe, respectful distance. They all take photos and videos.

A few minutes later, the whale shark moves away. It slowly disappears. You feel lucky to have seen such an amazing animal up close. It's an encounter of a lifetime!

THE END

To follow another path, turn to page 8.
To learn more about sharing the ocean, turn to page 101.

Not only are whale sharks bigger than other sharks, but they look very different. Their backs are covered with white spots. The patterns help camouflage the animal. The whale shark swims close. You can't help but reach out and touch it. It's so thrilling to touch a huge, wild animal!

After the dive is over, you excitedly tell the boat captain about the whale shark. To your shock, he gets angry! He explains that sharks have a coating on their skin. This coating protects the shark from bacteria in the water. Touching a whale shark could damage this coating and hurt the shark.

You feel terrible. You should have known better. You'll do better next time.

THE END

To follow another path, turn to page 8.
To learn more about sharing the ocean, turn to page 101.

Snorkeling is the right choice for this reef. Most of the reef is in shallow water. It's only about 100 feet deep in many places.

Some areas are even shallower than that. This lets in lots of sunlight. You can clearly see all the reef's beauty and life.

There are more than 1,500 species of fish and 400 species of coral in the Great Barrier Reef. It feels like they're all right here!

Brightly colored soft coral wave in the ocean current. Fish of every color drift past. You get out your underwater camera and take as many photos as you can.

Something shimmers in the water. It looks like a piece of floating glass. It's hard to tell what it might be.

Suddenly, it occurs to you. There's only one sea creature that's almost invisible in the water. That is a jellyfish. They are venomous, but most aren't deadly. You should be fine as long as you don't touch them. You wonder what kind of jellyfish this might be. Dare you risk taking a closer look?

• To investigate, turn to page 56.
• To explore another area, turn to page 61.

You slowly move close enough to see the outline of the jellyfish. It's a lot bigger than you thought. Its long tentacles stretch several feet behind it. They are almost invisible.

This is a box jellyfish. It's incredibly venomous! You notice several other flashes of light around you. With horror, you realize that you've swam into a swarm of box jellyfish.

It's hard to see how many there are because they're almost invisible. Your first instinct is to get away as fast as you can. But box jellyfish can swim, rather than just floating on the current like other jellyfish species. So maybe if you don't move, they'll leave you alone.

- To stay still, go to page 57.
- To swim away, turn to page 58.

You try not to panic and stay as still as possible. Without warning, burning pain hits your legs. You've been stung! You desperately swim for the boat. You feel stings on your arms and stomach as you go.

Once you get to the boat, the captain pours vinegar on the stings. It acts against the poison. Your legs, arms, and stomach become red and swollen. Red marks rise on your skin where the tentacles touched you. By the time you get to the hospital, you're vomiting. You can barely breathe. Not too long after, your heart stops. It's a tragic end to your dream vacation.

THE END

To follow another path, turn to page 8.
To learn more about sharing the ocean, turn to page 101.

Your heart is pounding. You carefully swim around the box jellyfish. Finally, you're away from the deadly swarm. You wait until your heartbeat returns to normal. Then you get back to exploring the coral reef.

Nearby, you spot a large green sea turtle. It's chomping down on a jellyfish! These turtles eat box jellyfish. Scientists think the turtles' tough skin protects it from jellyfish stings.

Another turtle appears. You're excited to see it catch a jellyfish, too. But it is making odd movements. Carefully, you swim closer. The turtle's back fins are caught in a tangle of fishing net. You could try to cut the net away yourself. Or you could go for help. But if you go for help, you may not be able to find the turtle when you come back.

• To cut off the net yourself, go to page 59.
• To go for help, turn to page 60.

You pull a small knife from your pack. Cautiously, you approach the turtle. It seems to understand that you're there to help. It doesn't try to swim away.

Quickly, you cut through the layers of knotted net. You're careful not to touch the animal itself. You know touching wild animals can be harmful to both you and them. Finally, the last piece of net comes free!

Then you see that the turtle is bleeding. The net has cut it in several places. It swims away, glad to be free. But you're not sure how long it will last in the wild. You hope it won't become a shark's next meal.

THE END

To follow another path, turn to page 8.
To learn more about sharing the ocean, turn to page 101.

The poor turtle is tired from fighting the net. It floats calmly nearby as you call for help.

Several crew members dive in. Together, you get the turtle onto the boat. Two of you cut the net away. The captain calls a turtle rescue group onshore. When the turtle rescuers arrive, they examine the turtle. It has several cuts from the nets. They agree to take it to the animal hospital. They will treat its wounds and care for it. Once it's healed and healthy, it can be released back into the ocean.

The rescuers thank you for your quick thinking. If it hadn't been for you, the turtle might have drowned. It feels good to have helped one of these beautiful ocean creatures.

THE END

To follow another path, turn to page 8.
To learn more about sharing the ocean, turn to page 101.

You're not taking any chances with jellyfish. Quickly, you move to another area of the reef.

You float on the ocean's surface. The reef spreads out below like a carpet of a thousand colors. Soft pink corals sway in the current beside hard purple, green, and orange corals. Fish of every color glide through the water.

You get some great photos. Now you want to get some selfies to send to your friends back home.

It's tough to get the right angle, though. You'd have to swim very close to the reef to get the shot. You don't want to step on the coral. It could damage the reef and kill the coral. Coral is also sharp too. You could be seriously injured if it cut you.

- To try to get the shot anyway, turn to page 62.
- To decide the photo isn't worth it, turn to page 64.

You position yourself beside the coral. You are careful to stand in a sandy area near the reef and not on any of the coral itself. The fish and the reef look perfect in the background. This is going to be your best photo of the trip! But just as you press the button, the ocean current pulls you forward.

It all happens so quickly. Without thinking, you step forward to keep your balance. Terrible pain shoots through your leg. At first, you think you have cut yourself on a rough coral rock. Then the rock moves!

It wasn't coral after all. It was a stonefish! Stonefish are one of the world's most venomous creatures. They live in coral reefs and camouflage themselves for protection. It stung you with its sharp venomous spines.

Others help you up the ladder and onto the deck. Your leg swells up and you pass out from the pain. Much later, you wake up in the hospital. Your dream vacation is ruined, all for a stupid picture. But you know you're lucky to be alive.

THE END

To follow another path, turn to page 8.
To learn more about sharing the ocean, turn to page 101.

Touching or taking the coral is against the rules. The coral reef is fragile. One wrong move could break a piece of coral and kill the organisms inside. Coral is also very sharp. You could injure yourself badly. None of that is worth a photo op. You find a few willing angelfish to take selfies with. Then you continue on your way.

At the end of the dive, everyone gathers on the boat for dinner. You all swap stories of the amazing things you saw. This is vacation of a lifetime. You'll never forget your amazing ocean encounters.

THE END

To follow another path, turn to page 8.
To learn more about sharing the ocean, turn to page 101.

CHAPTER 4

AN ARCTIC ADVENTURE

You've been interested in the Arctic all your life. There is something magical about the frozen places of the world. It's also been your dream to be a marine biologist. Now your dream has come true! You're part of a scientific expedition spending the summer in the Arctic. The team's focus is the ecosystem and the animals that live there.

• Turn the page.

Climate change has affected the area in many ways. Summers are warmer and last longer. This has allowed some animals to come here that have never lived in the Arctic before. For instance, one of the marine predators you hope to see are orcas, or killer whales. Orcas used to be rare in the Arctic. But now they can move into areas that were once frozen.

Once your team has settled in, it's time to get started. There have been no sightings of orcas nearby. So the team decides to focus on other research. One of the animals the team will study is the narwhal. You've heard reports of a narwhal pod a few miles away. You also plan to study humpback whales. There have been humpback whale sightings farther out at sea.

• To look for the narwhals, go to page 69.
• To search for the humpback whales, turn to page 86.

Narwhals are marine mammals. They live in the deep, cold waters of the Arctic. These mysterious ocean creatures breathe oxygen, like dolphins and whales.

Narwhals have the nickname "unicorn of the sea." This is because male narwhals grow long, thin tusks. The tusks look like unicorn horns. Narwhals hit their prey with the tusk. This stuns the fish. Then the narwhal can easily catch it.

You search the ocean surface for any sign of the narwhal pod. One reason they're so mysterious is that narwhals are very hard to find. Most of the year, they live in remote areas under thick ice. They are afraid of humans and of the sound of boats. But during the summer months, narwhals move south. There they find food and raise their young.

• Turn the page.

After several hours, you spot the pod! If you're quick, you can dive in and take a closer look. Or you can stay in the boat and watch them from a distance.

• To get into your scuba suit and dive, go to page 71.
• To stay in the boat, turn to page 80.

It might be summer, but the Arctic Ocean is still cold. You pull on a thick wetsuit and gloves. A diving mask covers your whole face to protect your skin.

The shock of the cold hits hard when you slip into the water. You swim toward the area where you had spotted the narwhals. Soon, you see a large shape appear. It's a male narwhal. You know it's a male because it has a tusk.

Curious, the narwhal glides toward you. It swims so close that you can see its eyes calmly checking you out. Its gray skin is covered with white spots. This helps to camouflage it in the murky Arctic water.

Several more narwhals appear. They swim slowly in circles, gently touching tusks. This behavior is called "tusking." It's a way the narwhals communicate with each other.

• Turn the page.

Suddenly, the whole group swims away toward the shoreline. It would probably be safer to observe them from the boat. But you could also stay in the water and try to swim to catch up.

• To swim to the boat, go to page 73.
• To swim after the narwhals, turn to page 75.

You scramble onto the deck and search for any sign of the narwhals. Soon, you spot them. They're a little farther up the shoreline.

The narwhals seem to be in a panic. The animals are frantically crowding each other. They're splashing and tossing their tusks in the air.

Then you see a flash of black and white lunge out of the water. It's an orca! Several more of these huge killer whales rush by. They leap out of the water with breathtaking speed.

Orcas aren't actually whales at all. They're the largest members of the dolphin family. Orcas in the wild have never killed a human. But killing their prey is another thing. Orcas are one of the ocean's most deadly predators.

• Turn the page.

Your heart pounds as you scan the water for signs of blood. But before the orcas get too close, the narwhals rush away and disappear. Narwhals swim fast. They can dive very deep down into the cold water. The orcas swim in circles, looking for their prey. Then they disappear as well.

It was exciting to see a group of orcas hunting together. But you're glad the narwhals got away. What an incredible way to start your expedition!

THE END

To follow another path, turn to page 8.
To learn more about sharing the ocean, turn to page 101.

Eventually, you manage to catch up to the pod. You don't even consider any possible danger to you. These animals are fascinating! They're crowding together, their tusks clacking loudly. You have never heard of narwhals swimming this close to shore before.

Suddenly, you feel a sharp pain in your shoulder, and you see blood in the water. Your blood. A tusk must have cut you. You don't think it's too bad, though.

Suddenly, a huge black and white shape appears. It's an orca! These killer whales are at the top of the food chain. You know they don't attack humans. But they do eat many kinds of marine animals, including narwhals. These orcas are hunting. And you're caught in the middle.

• Turn the page.

You've got to figure out a way to escape before you're trapped in a deadly attack. Your shoulder is starting to hurt, making swimming more difficult. The shore is closer. But to get there, you'd have to swim through the pod of terrified narwhals. You could try to swim to the boat. But you would risk getting caught up in the deadly hunt.

• To dodge through the narwhal pod toward shore, go to page 77.
• To swim to the boat—directly into the orca's path, turn to page 78.

By now, the narwhals are in full panic. They're pushing and bumping each other, trying to get away. There must be more than one orca out there for this pod to be so terrified. You see an opening between two narwhals. You head toward it. But your injured shoulder slows you down. You don't make it through. Several narwhals pile together around you. They squeeze tight, frantically swimming forward and taking you with them.

A powerful shove knocks your mouthpiece away. You gasp for air, but nothing but cold salt water enters your lungs. After the narwhals speed away, your team finds your lifeless body washed up on the beach.

THE END

To follow another path, turn to page 8.
To learn more about sharing the ocean, turn to page 101.

You need to get to the safety of the boat! Suddenly the orcas speed past. Luckily, they don't seem to notice you. They're working as a team to trap the narwhal pod. They put themselves between the narwhals and the open sea. Then they close in on the narwhals like a net.

This kind of hunting behavior is what you hoped to see on this research trip. But you hadn't counted on being part of the hunt! Painfully, you swim toward the boat.

Finally, you make it back. Everyone on board is frantic with excitement. They've been watching the action in the water. The team is too excited to notice that you're bleeding. You didn't realize how bad you were injured. The world gets fuzzy, then goes dark.

Sometime later, you wake up with a bandaged shoulder. The captain says you got stabbed by a narwhal tusk. It will be a few days before you can get back to work. But at least you escaped the orca attack. The narwhals weren't so lucky.

THE END

To follow another path, turn to page 8.
To learn more about sharing the ocean, turn to page 101.

The narwhals begin to behave strangely.
The pod heads toward the shore, crowding
together. Their tusks keep popping out of the
water. Something extraordinary is happening,
but you're not sure what.

Then without warning, you see several black dorsal fins rise out of the waves. They're moving toward the pod. Orcas!

You watch in amazement as the orcas race toward the narwhals. You know orcas hunt as a group, but you've never watched it before. It's one of the things you had hoped to see on this trip.

The scientific team has heard stories of orcas hunting narwhals. But no one has ever recorded it. Until recently, orcas rarely came this far north. The Arctic ice was too dangerous for the orcas. The sharp ice could cut the orcas' dorsal fins. But now, because of climate change, the summer Arctic ice melts faster. Orcas can safely travel farther north than they ever have.

• Turn the page.

This is bad news for narwhals. Narwhals don't have many natural predators. Orcas are a new threat. Narwhals aren't used to being hunted by orcas. An orca attack like this one confuses and panics the narwhals.

The lead scientist wants to get closer to the hunt. She decides to send a small inflatable boat toward the action.

You want to get closer too. But you're worried about your safety. It might be safer to videotape the event from the boat. Will a small inflatable be tough enough to withstand an orca attack?

• To stay on the boat, go to page 83.
• To go on the small inflatable, turn to page 84.

You grab the team's video camera and start recording the orcas. They lunge toward the narwhal pod. Fins and tusks thrash in the churning water. A few seconds later, all the animals disappear. The water is calm but tinted dark pink. The orcas circle and dive, and you know what they're doing. They're feeding.

Later that evening, everyone eagerly watches your video of the attack. No one on the team had seen orcas attack a pod of narwhals. Now thanks to you, they can watch it over and over. It's an exciting start to the summer. You can't wait to see what else you'll see.

THE END

To follow another path, turn to page 8.
To learn more about sharing the ocean, turn to page 101.

You are thrilled as the inflatable is lowered from the boat. You stop the raft a safe distance away. You even drop an underwater camera over the side. Hopefully, it will capture some of the orcas' behavior.

Without warning, a huge black orca appears in the water a few feet away. Something hits the boat from below! At first, you think the orca is attacking. Then a long tusk pops up from the surface. You realize it's the narwhals making a frantic escape.

There's no time to get away. You hang on and hope the animals don't flip the raft. The narwhals dive deep and get away. The orcas dive and resurface. Then they give up and disappear.

You pull up the underwater camera. It's gone. It must have torn away when the narwhals hit the raft. Disappointed, you head back to the boat. You hope you didn't just blow your only chance to film orcas during your summer in the Arctic.

THE END

To follow another path, turn to page 8.
To learn more about sharing the ocean, turn to page 101.

It's a beautiful morning to look for humpback whales. You bundle up and set off on the research boat.

Humpback whales live in all the world's major oceans. They spend the winter months in warm tropical waters. There they mate and give birth to their young. In the summer, the whales travel thousands of miles to feeding grounds in the Arctic.

A few miles offshore, you have your first sighting. You pull out your binoculars and watch the whales. They swim lazily, their tail fins popping out of the water as they dive.

Every whale has a different color pattern on its tail fin. Scientists use these markings to identify individual whales. Another scientist on the team recognizes several tail patterns. These whales have been coming to this area for many years.

Several of the females have their babies with them. It's exciting to see so many baby whales! You'd like to get some video of the whales and their young. An underwater shot would be amazing. But you don't want to disturb them, either.

- To dive with the whales, turn to page 88.
- To stay on the boat, turn to page 94.

Humpback whales are gentle creatures, but they are huge. These giants can grow up to 50 feet long. They weigh more than 40 tons. Mother whales are very protective of their young. A close encounter could be deadly.

Carefully, you slip into the water. You swim toward the whales. They're peacefully moving through the water. They roll gently and circle each other. It's like they are dancing. You stop a safe distance away to watch.

Then strange, haunting sounds begin. The whales are singing. Long, deep notes, clicks, squeaks, and moans fill the water. You've never been this close to humpback whales when they were singing.

You're so focused on the whales that you don't see an enormous shape rise from below. You look down and gasp. It's a shark!

You can't tell what kind of shark it is yet. Should you stay still and hope it ignores you, or should you try to get back to the boat before it gets too close?

• To stay still and watch the shark, turn to page 90.
• To go back to the boat, turn to page 92.

You don't think you'd have time to get back to the boat, so you freeze and watch. As the shark swims closer, you see that it's a Greenland shark. They live in the cold, deep areas of the Arctic. Because they live in such deep water, they haven't been well studied.

Greenland sharks are some of the biggest sharks in the world. They can grow more than 15 feet long. These sharks can live to be more than 270 years old!

Greenland sharks are also slow swimmers, so you're not worried that you're in danger. They're also almost totally blind. But that doesn't keep them from being a top ocean predator. These sharks eat many ocean animals, including squid and seals. They also take big bites out of other animals such as beluga whales.

It's so rare to see a Greenland shark that you immediately start filming. It swims slowly past you. Then it gently disappears back down.

You return to the boat thrilled. You excitedly tell the team what you saw. The team makes plans to drop some deep-water cameras here. Hopefully, you'll get another chance to study this rare ocean animal. Today's surprise encounter is one you'll never forget.

THE END

To follow another path, turn to page 8.
To learn more about sharing the ocean, turn to page 101.

You're not sure what kind of shark it was, but you don't take any chances. Back on the boat, you and the team continue to watch the humpback whales. You record the songs to listen to later. Each whale has its own sounds, so you hope to match the sounds with each whale.

The whales stay in this area for several hours. They feed and sing. One way humpbacks hunt is by what's called bubble-net feeding. The whales spot a school of fish. One whale blows a huge circle of bubbles around the school. The bubble is like a net. It traps the fish. The other whales push the trapped fish toward the surface. Then the whales race upward with their mouths open. They explode out of the water and swallow as many fish as they can. It's an amazing sight to see.

Finally, the whales move on. It's time to return to base camp. It's been an amazing first day and you look forward to what you'll see for the rest of the summer.

THE END

To follow another path, turn to page 8.
To learn more about sharing the ocean, turn to page 101.

You don't want to stress the whales, so you stay on the boat. After an hour or so, the whales move away. The team decides to head farther out to sea.

Suddenly, one massive whale launches itself out of the water. It twists and flaps its huge fins. Then it crashes down, making a huge splash. This jumping is called breaching, and humpback whales love to do it. Scientists think breaching is a type of communication between whales.

For the next hour, the whales breach. The team is amazed at this display. Even the baby whales get into the act, learning to breach like their mothers. Eventually, the group swims away.

As the boat heads back toward the research camp, you glimpse a flash of white in the water. Chances are good that this is a pod of beluga whales. It's another animal your team wants to study.

You didn't sleep well last night, and you'd like to get back to base camp. But you might never get a chance to see beluga whales again. On the other hand, the flash of white could have been nothing.

• To keep looking for beluga whales, turn to page 96.
• To go back to camp, turn to page 98.

Belugas are small, white whales. They look like pale ghosts in the water. You're here, so you might as well get some good underwater footage.

Quickly, you pull on your scuba gear and drop into the water. Beluga whales are social animals. They circle you curiously. They bump the camera playfully with their heads. Like many Arctic marine animals, belugas have no fin on their backs. This adaptation lets them swim amid ice and not injure themselves.

Belugas also have unique heads with a large bump called a melon. The melon can change shape and allow the whale to have different facial expressions. The whales look like they're grinning as they swim around you.

After a few minutes, they drift away. Excited, you return to the boat and show everyone your video. Swimming with the whales was definitely a great start to a great summer. It was totally worth staying in the water longer!

THE END

To follow another path, turn to page 8.
To learn more about sharing the ocean, turn to page 101.

You're almost back to base camp when one of the team members shouts excitedly. A pod of dolphins has surrounded the boat! You identify them as white-beaked dolphins.

Most people think dolphins only live in tropical waters. But these dolphins live in cold north Atlantic areas. They don't usually come this far north, however. Though you're exhausted, you know that seeing them here is a rare treat.

White-beaked dolphins are very social animals. They travel in large pods. The dolphins jump out of the water as they race beside the boat. Some of them "surf" the wake behind the boat. They swim with you for several miles. Everyone excitedly watches the dolphins. Some take pictures, and you videotape them.

Eventually, the creatures disappear beneath the water. The boat turns back toward the dock. There is something magical about a dolphin encounter. You hope you'll see them again this summer.

THE END

To follow another path, turn to page 8.
To learn more about sharing the ocean, turn to page 101.

CHAPTER 5

SAFELY SHARING THE OCEAN

Humans have had thousands of encounters with wild ocean animals. But until recently, few of them had been filmed. Today, the internet is filled with footage of extraordinary encounters with ocean animals.

Many of these videos make the animals seem more threatening than they are. Or they show people deliberately upsetting an animal so it will fight back. The reality of these videos is that even the deadliest ocean animals don't usually attack humans.

Attacks are usually the result of an animal being afraid or in pain. Rarely do they harm a human for no reason.

Take sharks, for example. When we think "deadly ocean predator," the first animal that comes to mind is a shark. It is true that some sharks attack humans, but it is very rare.

People are much more dangerous to sharks. Humans fish for sharks for their skin, teeth, and fins. More than 100 million sharks are killed every year.

The world's oceans need sharks. Sharks are apex predators. They are at the top of the ocean food chain. Sharks prey on other fish and on weaker animals. This keeps the ocean ecosystems like coral reefs healthy and in balance.

Or how about orcas, or killer whales? Their name says it all. Or does it? Orcas kill a lot of ocean animals, including dolphins, seals, whales, and even sharks. Wild orcas don't kill people, though. They get their name from the way they hunt and kill their prey.

Orcas are very social animals that are curious about humans. In 2018, a woman in New Zealand got the experience of a lifetime. A family of orcas came to play and swim with her.

Many other divers have recorded their gentle encounters with orcas. These encounters show that orcas are not a threat to people.

Seeing wild ocean creatures can be an unforgettable experience. There are basic, common sense rules when encountering an ocean animal.

The most important thing to remember is to give the animals plenty of space. Boats should stay at least 100 yards (91 meters) away from whales, dolphins, or other sea creatures.

Divers should never try to touch or pet the animals. Don't chase animals or try to follow them. Keep away from mothers and their young. Don't feed the animals.

By following these rules, most people who interact with ocean animals can have a thrilling encounter that is safe for everyone.

Nan Hauser

In 2018, marine biologist Nan Hauser was diving near the Cook Islands. Suddenly, an enormous humpback whale appeared near her. To her surprise, the whale tried to lift her out of the water. He covered her with his fins and rolled in the water beside her. Then Hauser realized there was a huge tiger shark nearby! Hauser is convinced the whale was saving her from the shark. It's the first time a humpback whale has been seen to protect a human.

Texas Turtles

In February 2021, a winter storm hit South Padre Island, Texas. As the temperatures dropped, thousands of sea turtles became "cold stunned" by the low temperatures. Cold-stunned turtles become paralyzed. They can't swim. People heard about the turtles. They went out in their own boats to rescue them. So many turtles needed help that the city's convention center was opened to hold them all.

More than 12,000 sea turtles had been affected by the storm. When the turtles and the temperatures warmed up, volunteers came back to help release them into the wild.

Syna Family

In the summer of 2021, the Syna family took their boat out into Puget Sound in Washington state. There they had an unexpected encounter with a killer whale. The huge animal suddenly appeared and rubbed its nose against their boat. The friendly orca started playing by circling the boat, then swimming under it. After a few minutes, the orca left and the family decided to go home. But the orca wasn't done yet! It came back and followed the family until the boat reached shore, then it swam away.

Safely swimming with wild ocean animals can be thrilling! But how do companies find dolphins and other wildlife for customers to see them? Sometimes they take tourists to areas where the animals are feeding or migrating. This can upset the animals. It might also damage the environment. Some people argue that careful tour companies don't hurt the animals. They say these programs are a safe, educational way to teach kids about ocean wildlife. Would you be a part of a program like this? Why or why not?

Ocean parks around the world offer entertainment shows that feature captive ocean animals. These same parks also have programs that help wild animals. Some people say these parks take good care of the animals. The shows make many people want to protect the animals. Others say that all ocean animals should be set free. Do you think it is fair to keep these animals in captivity? Why or why not?

Some beach swimming areas are protected by shark nets. These nets allow beaches to attract more visitors. But they also have a downside. Shark nets catch other large ocean animals such as dolphins and turtles. Often, these animals drown when they're caught in the nets. Do you think these nets are a good thing or a bad thing? Why or why not?

apex [AY-peks]—the top of, the peak

barracuda [bar-uh-KOO-duh]—a long, tropical predator fish

camouflage [KAM-uh-flahzh]—to hide something by changing how it looks

dorsal [DAWR-suhl]—the fin on the back of a fish

endangered [en-DAYN-jerd]—at risk of dying out

expedition [ek-spi-DISH-uhn]—a journey made for a special reason

fleet [fleet]—a large group of ships

goliath [guh-LAHY-uhth]—a very large person or thing

infection [in-FEK-shun]—a disease in part of a person's body that is caused by germs or bacteria

invasive [in-VAY-siv]—posing a threat by invading

plankton [PLANGK-tuhn]—microscopic organisms floating in the ocean

predator [PRED-uh-ter]—an animal that preys on other animals

venomous [VEN-uh-muhs]—an animal that can give a poisoned bite or sting

BIBLIOGRAPHY

Florida Museum
floridamuseum.ufl.edu

National Geographic
nationalgeographic.com

NOAA Fisheries
fisheries.noaa.gov

Oceana
oceana.org

Ocean Conservancy
oceanconservancy.org

World Wildlife Fund
worldwildlife.org

READ MORE

Davies, Nicola. *Ocean Monsters: Interact with Lifesize Sea Predators!* UK: Carlton Kids Books, 2017.

Erickson, Paul. *Don't Mess With Me: The Strange Lives of Venomous Sea Creatures.* ME: Tilbury House Publishers, 2018.

Lassieur, Allison. *Can You Survive Deadly Rain Forest Encounters?* North Mankato, MN: Capstone, 2023.

INTERNET SITES

Dive and Discover: Expeditions to the Seafloor
divediscover.whoi.edu

Everything Oceans
kids.nationalgeographic.com/videos/topic/everything-oceans

Monterey Bay Aquarium
montereybayaquarium.org

Allison Lassieur is an award-winning author of more than 150 history and nonfiction books about everything from Ancient Rome to the International Space Station. Her books have received several Kirkus starred reviews and Booklist recommendations, and her historical novel *Journey to a Promised Land* was awarded the 2020 Kansas Library Association Notable Book Award and Library of Congress Great Reads Book selection. Allison lives in upstate New York with her husband, daughter, a scruffy, lovable mutt named Jingle Jack, and more books than she can count.